IT'S A FACT

Wacky Bible

BLOCK HEADS

I can't
believe it!

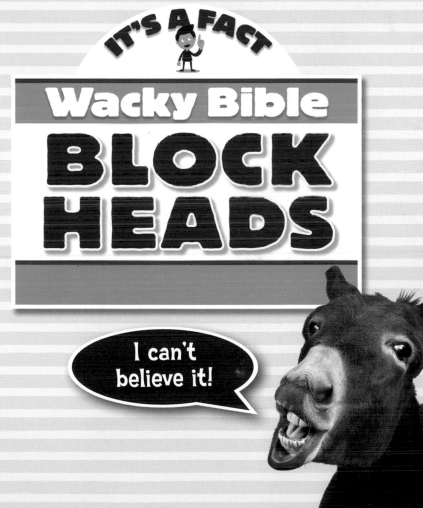

It's a fact!

ZONDERKIDZ

Wacky Bible Blockheads
Copyright © 2014 by ZonderKidz

Requests for information should be addressed to:
ZonderKidz, 3900 *Sparks Drive, Grand Rapids, Michigan* 49546

Library of Congress Cataloging-in-Publication Data

Wacky Bible Blockheads : completely, 100%, historically accurate.
    pages cm. -- (It's a fact)
    ISBN 978-0-310-74419-1 (softcover)
    1. Bible stories, English--Juvenile literature. 2. Bible--
Biography--Juvenile literature. 3. Bible--Miscellanea--Juvenile
literature.
BS551.3.W25 2014
220.95'05--dc23   2013024683

Editor: Kim Childress
Contributors: Kim Childress, Alyssa Helm, Andrea Vinley Jewel,
Kelly White, Megan Alexander
Cover and interior design: Kris Nelson/StoryLook Design
Photos: istock, Shutterstock, Thinkstock

Printed in China

14 15 16 17 18 /DSC/ 12 11 10 9 8 7 6 5 4 3 2 1

TABLE OF CONTENTS

Also in the series:

IT'S A FACT Wacky Bible Gross Outs

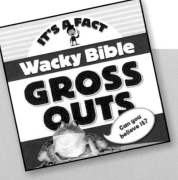

section	title	page

section	title	page

section	title	page

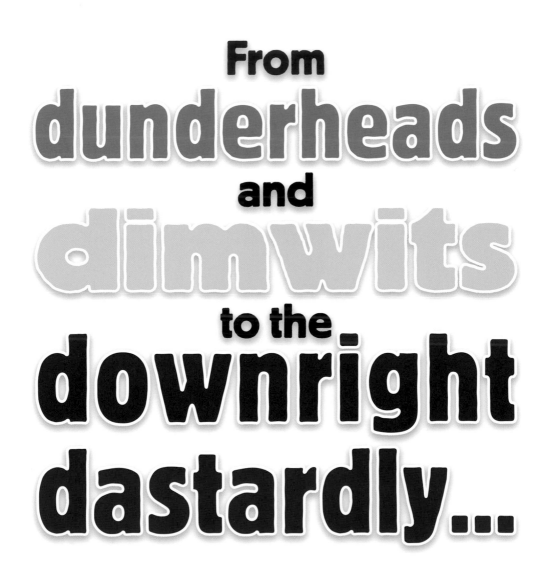

The Bible is full of folks who had "**duh**" moments.

There were good guys who made mistakes, people corrupted by power or greed, and even all-out evildoers who wanted to take everyone down. In these pages you'll meet lots of characters who've **fumbled** and **stumbled.**

DOUBLE THE
TROUBLE
COUPLES

BEGINNER BLOCKHEADS
101

The first-ever blockheads of the Bible were, well, the first man and woman— **ADAM AND EVE.** Eve fell for the scheming of a sneaky serpent, who talked her into making a snack out of a particular fruit that had been FORBIDDEN BY GOD. And Adam munched right along with her. THE RESULT?

The two now knew
EVIL

where before they only knew GOODNESS, and so they got evicted from THEIR PARADISE in the Garden of Eden.

The city of
Sodom
had become
Sin Central,
so it was destroyed by a rainstorm of
burning sulfur.

But God promised Abraham that his cousin

LOT would be spared.

Despite warnings from God's angels to

GET OUT
NOW!

You are now leaving Sin City.

Lot was reluctant to leave.

On the way out of Sodom, Lot's wife looked back at the smoldering city and turned into a pillar of **SALT.**

AFTER JESUS' RESURRECTION, all believers were of one heart and mind, so they shared everything they had. But **ANANIAS AND HIS WIFE SAPPHIRA** tried to hold back. They'd sold a valuable piece of property and **POCKETED** some of the CASH for themselves.

When asked by the apostles, Ananias said that was all the money they got.

LIE! Ananias fell down and died right there.

THREE HOURS LATER ...

UNAWARE OF WHAT JUST HAPPENED TO HER HUSBAND, SAPPHIRA TOLD THE SAME STORY TO THE APOSTLES.

LIE!

Sapphira fell down and died right there.

ANANIAS

SAPPHIRA

DAVID was the underdog, the smallest and youngest of eight sons. After killing Goliath, the Philistine giant, with just a rock and a slingshot, David became a great soldier and then a beloved king.

KING DAVID'S BIG MISTAKE?

One day, he looked down from the palace and saw Bathsheba, a married woman, taking a bath. David then plotted to have Bathsheba's husband killed so he could marry her.

David was genuinely sorry for his wrong and asked God for forgiveness. God forgave him and gave David many descendants, including … Jesus! David's story shows that no sin is too big for God to forgive.

Dear God,

You already know this but I really, majorly messed up!

Super sorry,
King David

God blessed **ABRAHAM** with a beautiful wife named **SARAH.** When they moved to **EGYPT,** Abraham lied and said Sarah was his sister. Instead of trusting God, Abraham feared he'd be killed if **HEAD-HONCHO PHARAOH** knew the truth.

Of course, Pharaoh fell in love with sarah at first sight and added her to his harem.

OOPS!

Even though Pharaoh didn't know the truth about Sarah, GOD CURSED HIM for taking another man's wife. Pharaoh figured out this was the reason he and his household had been inflicted with diseases, so HE SENT SARAH BACK TO ABRAHAM.

Abraham made the same mistake again

when he moved to a place called Gerar and said Sarah was his sister. King Abimelek tried to take Sarah into his harem.

God appeared

to King Abimelek **in a dream,** to tell him Sarah was married. Abimelek was quick to respond and asked for forgiveness when he sent Sarah back to Abraham.

Like father, like son.

Abraham's son, Isaac, married a beautiful woman name Rebekah. They moved to the land of the Philistines, where King Abimelek still ruled, and Issac lied and said Rebekah was his sister.

During the rebuilding of Jerusalem,

after the city had been **DESTROYED** by the Babylonians, an enemy of the Jews named **SANBALLAT** constantly **THREATENED**, **HARASSED**, and **INSULTED** the Jews as they worked. Sanballat sent a message to the prophet **NEHEMIAH**, who was overseeing the project.

Dear Nehemiah,

Word on the street is that you and the Jews are plotting to revolt. Is that why you're building the wall?

Yours truly,
Sanballat

x 5

Persistent (and fearful) fellow that he was, Sanballat sent the message FIVE times before Nehemiah finally responded.

Dear Sanballat,

What, are you paranoid? It's all in your head.

Sincerely,
Nehemiah

ZECHARIAH was offering incense in the temple when the **ANGEL GABRIEL** appeared to him. Gabriel told him his wife, Elizabeth, would **GIVE BIRTH TO A SON,** even though she was very old. Zechariah didn't believe Gabriel, so Gabriel proclaimed that Zechariah would **LOSE HIS VOICE** until the baby was born.

GABRIEL ALSO SAID,
"AND YOU ARE TO CALL THE BABY JOHN."

In Bible times, most babies were named after a family member. But once the baby was born, Elizabeth said, **"HE IS TO BE CALLED JOHN."**

"That can't be," neighbors and relatives replied. "John is not a family name."

But Zechariah took out a writing tablet and wrote, "His name is John." At that moment, the Lord **OPENED ZECHARIAH'S MOUTH** and he was able to to speak again.

Moral of the story:

DON'T ARGUE WITH ANGELS.

SIBLING RIVALRY?

CAIN AND ABEL were the sons of Adam and Eve, but Cain felt **OUTSHINED** by Abel.

POP QUIZ

HOW DID CAIN DEAL WITH HIS JEALOUSY OF ABEL?

A. HE HID ABEL'S BEST SHEEP.

B. HE KILLED ABEL'S BEST SHEEP.

C. HE KILLED ABEL'S WHOLE FLOCK OF SHEEP.

D. HE KILLED ABEL.

ANSWER: D) INSTEAD OF CONTROLLING HIS ANGER, CAIN LURED ABEL OUT INTO A FIELD AND MURDERED HIM! AS A RESULT, GOD CURSED CAIN—TAKING AWAY HIS ABILITY TO FARM AND TURNING HIM INTO A FUGITIVE FOR LIFE.

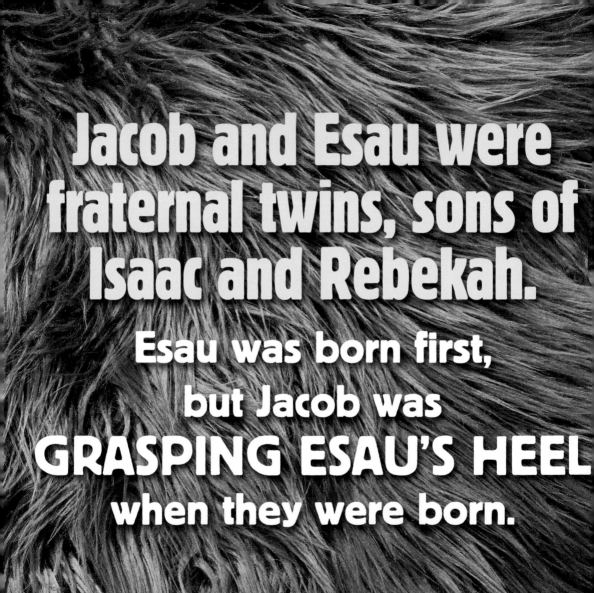

Jacob and Esau were fraternal twins, sons of Isaac and Rebekah.

Esau was born first, but Jacob was **GRASPING ESAU'S HEEL** when they were born.

When Esau was born, his whole body was covered in **RED HAIR**. He had so much hair that the Bible describes him as a hairy garment—like a **FUR COAT.**

Esau's brother, Jacob, was definitely a trickster!

Turn the page to find out why.

The name

JACOB

in ancient Hebrew

can mean,

"One who follows,"

or

"One who cheats."

One day, Esau returned home from hunting, and he was TIRED and HUNGRY. He asked Jacob for food. Jacob said yes, but for a price.

Esau: I'm hungry! Hand it over.

Jacob: First, give me your birthright.

Jacob tricked Esau into giving up his rights as the firstborn son.

And Esau sold his birthright—his place as firstborn of the family—for a bowl of beans!

EVEN MORE TRICKS!

WHEN ISAAC WAS OLD and couldn't see, as he was lying on his deathbed, he told Esau, **"SON, GO HUNT SOME WILD GAME** and prepare it for me the way I like it. Then I'll give you MY BLESSING before I die."

REBEKAH overheard this, so while Esau was out hunting, she SCHEMED to intercept that blessing for Jacob.

She prepared **TASTY FOOD** for Isaac, just the way he liked it. She **DRESSED JACOB** in **ESAU'S BEST CLOTHES** and covered his neck and arms in **GOAT FUR** to mimic Esau's hairy skin. When Jacob delivered Isaac's food, **ISAAC WAS FOOLED** and gave Esau's **BLESSING** to Jacob.

His sons, HOPHNI AND PHINEHAS, also priests, were well-known around town as SCOUNDRELS. They REBELLED against God's rules and STOLE offerings meant for God. Eli WARNED Hophni and Phinehas that their sins were so bad that no one would PRAY on their behalf.

GOD WARNED ELI

that he would KILL BOTH SONS on the same day. Sure enough, during a battle with the Philistines, HOPHNI AND PHINEHAS DIED. When Eli heard the news, he fell backward in his chair, BROKE HIS NECK, and also died.

What was it about King David's boys? They all wanted a piece of the throne.

Step aside,
Adonijah. I'm
the new king.

While David was dying, his son, Adonijah proclaimed himself king and was already celebrating with his buddies.

But David's wife, Bathsheba, quickly set the record straight. Her son, Solomon, would be king. So David cleared up the misunderstanding and proclaimed Solomon the next king:

"Long live King Solomon!"

And just like that, Adonijah's victory party was over.

DREAM BOY

JOSEPH WAS ONE OF JACOB'S TWELVE SONS. BECAUSE HE WAS JACOB'S FAVORITE, HE GAVE JOSEPH A MULTI-COLORED ROBE, WHICH SYMBOLIZED A POSITION OF HONOR. WHEN JOSEPH'S BROTHERS SAW THAT ROBE, THEY HATED JOSEPH.

JOSEPH ALSO TOLD HIS BROTHERS ABOUT HIS STRANGE DREAMS IN WHICH THEY ALL BOWED DOWN TO HIM. THEY HATED HIM EVEN MORE AND PLOTTED WAYS TO GET RID OF HIM.

Joseph's brothers conspired together and sold Joseph into Egyptian slavery.

FOR SALE!
ONE BROTHER, AGE 17
ANSWERS TO THE NAME
"JOSEPH"
COST: 20 SHEKELS OF SILVER
COAT NOT INCLUDED

SO THEY TORE HIS COLORFUL COAT, AND SMEARED IT WITH GOAT'S BLOOD, THEN GAVE IT TO THEIR FATHER, JACOB, AND TOLD HIM JOSEPH WAS KILLED BY A WILD ANIMAL.

JOSEPH'S BROTHERS
thought they were rid of him,
BUT THEY DIDN'T KNOW
he had become the

EGYPTIAN PHARAOH'S
SECOND IN COMMAND!

When they came to Egypt for food during a famine, they bowed down before Joseph.

JOSEPH'S DREAM HAD COME TRUE!

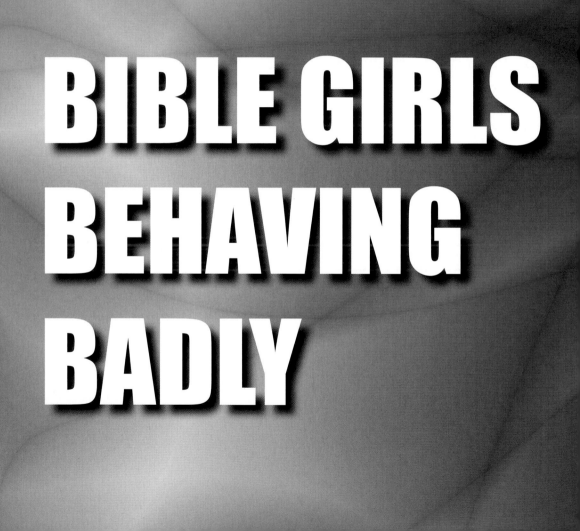

Official Court Transcripts

Mom No. 1 vs. Mom No. 2
Presiding Judge: King Solomon

Mom No. 1: Pardon me, king. This woman and I live in the same house, and we both had baby boys. During the night, her baby died. So while I was asleep, she took my boy and put hers next to me. The following morning, I got up—and my baby was dead! But I looked at him closely in the morning light and saw that it was her baby.

Mom No. 2: No! The living one is my baby; the dead one is yours.

Mom No. 1: No! The dead one is yours; the living one is mine.

King Solomon: Bring me a sword. Cut the living baby in two, and give half to one mother and half to the other.

Mom No. 1: Don't kill him! Please! Give her the baby!

Mom No. 2: Nope. Cut him in two!

King Solomon: Don't kill the baby! Give him to the first woman. She is his mother.

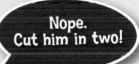

Would this baby's real mother please stand up?

King Solomon knew Mom No. 2 wasn't the real mom when she boldly agreed to split the baby.

Don't kill him! Please! Give the baby to her!

Nope. Cut him in two!

59

AHAB,

KING OF ISRAEL,

was married to a controlling wife named

JEZEBEL.

She wanted the people of Israel to worship gods like Baal, so she had many of the prophets of God put to death. God took that seriously, and Baal's 450 prophets were killed in a showdown.

JEZEBEL

continued her pursuit of power by

TRYING TO KILL

God's great prophet, Elijah.

She failed, and

GOD'S JUDGEMENT

fell upon her and Ahab. They both died, and

DOGS AND BIRDS

ate their bodies.

I can't believe it!

GRUESOME GRANNY

Queen Athaliah was the only woman
to reign over Judah,
a post she held for six years.

How wicked was she?

After her son, King Ahaziah,
was killed, she ordered
all of her grandsons killed, so she
could take the throne.

Athaliah's youngest grandson

escaped with the help of his aunt.

When the child was later

crowned king, Athaliah

heard crowds cheering

and went into the temple to see what

all the fuss was about. At the order of

the priest, **she was killed** as soon as

she left the temple.

I don't believe it!

Dear Grandpa,

Happy

BIRTHDAY

★ TO YOU ★

I hope you like the party!
Love, Herodias

Off with his head!

At Herod the Great's birthday party, his granddaughter, Herodias, danced for him so well that he said, "**MAKE A REQUEST, ANYTHING YOU WANT.**"

Her mother told her to ask for JOHN THE BAPTIST'S head on a platter.

And that's exactly what she got.

BULLIES ON THE BLOCK

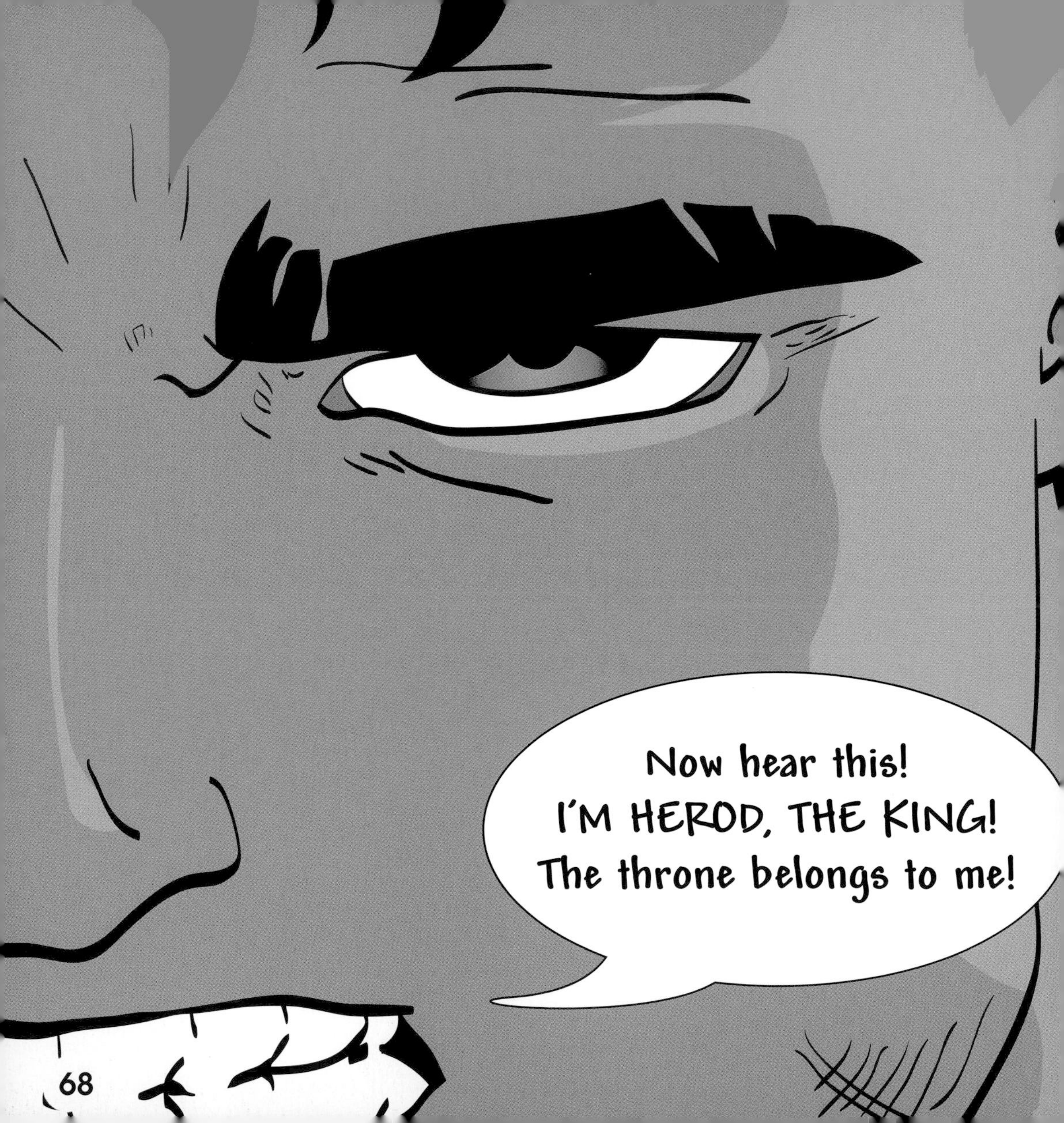
Now hear this!
I'M HEROD, THE KING!
The throne belongs to me!

JESUS WAS BORN DURING KING HEROD'S REIGN OVER JUDEA. THIS KING DIDN'T WANT ANYONE TAKING HIS CROWN, BUT HE KEPT HEARING ABOUT A BABY BEING BORN WHO WOULD BECOME KING OF THE JEWS.

Herod tried to give the three wise men the shakedown for information about the location of Jesus' birth, but they refused to spill the goods.

Herod's harebrained solution to protect his throne? Oh, he'd just have all the baby boys in the area killed. That'd take care of it—or so he thought!

Jesus lives!

FOUR HUNDRED YEARS

after Joseph died, a new Egyptian pharaoh feared the Israelites would start an uprising and take over his kingdom. So he enslaved them and ordered all infant boys to be killed.

But God had a plan, and he brought Moses to the rescue.

Through Moses, God brought ten plagues to Egypt before pharaoh finally agreed to let God's people go.

THE PLAGUES:

1. BLOOD
2. FROGS
3. GNATS
4. FLIES
5. LIVESTOCK DYING
6 BOILS
7. HAIL
8. LOCUSTS
9. DARKNESS
10. DEATH TO EVERY FIRST BORN SON

Why did this stubborn Pharaoh take so long to give in?

Pharaoh was used to getting his own way, and it would have been a sign of weakness to cave in to the wishes of his people—especially the Hebrew slaves. He figured he didn't have to answer to anyone, so he could break a promise to Moses.

Even after the **PLAGUES** had so completely ravaged Egypt, Pharaoh **DUG IN HIS HEELS** and was more determined than ever to keep his grip on the Israelites—that is, until the tenth plague. God took Pharaoh's **FIRSTBORN SON**—and the first son of all Egyptians and their animals.

PHARAOH WAS STUBBORN AS A MULE.

GOLIATH was a giant, over ELEVEN FEET TALL, and champion of the Philistine army.

But he let his strength go to his head, thinking he was even greater than God. He taunted the Israelites over and over.

Goliath laughed at David's challenge. David wasn't even old enough to be in the army. But Goliath's physical strength was no match for David's strong faith. God was with David, who took out the giant with a slingshot and stone in one pop!

FIRED UP!

King Nebuchadnezzar of Babylon erected a huge hunk of towering gold and ordered all the people to worship it.

But three Israelites named SHADRACH, MESHACH, and ABEDNEGO refused to bow down. King Nebuchadnezzar told them if they didn't worship his statue, they would be thrown immediately into a blazing furnace. "Then what god will rescue you from my hand?" the king asked.

So SHADRACH, MESHACH, and ABEDNEGO were thrown into the fire—ALIVE! The king and his people watched as an angel of God protected the three from burning up, and they walked out of the furnace—STILL ALIVE!

What happened to the king?

For a while Nebuchadnezzar FOLLOWED God closely, but he then got PUFFED UP with his own pride again, so God cursed him with craziness. He lost his mind and wound up living in FIELDS like a wild ANIMAL and eating grass.

KNUCKLEHEADS FOR KINGS

King Solomon was wise and respected as one of the greatest kings. But he had one shortcoming—or rather, **ONE THOUSAND.**

He had **SEVEN HUNDRED** wives and **THREE HUNDRED** mistresses.

And these women led him astray by convincing him to worship **FALSE GODS** and build shrines to their IDOLS.

BURNED!

The Bible had its share of foolish kings, and Jehoiakim was one of them.

When the scribe Jeremiah sent
KING JEHOIAKIM OF JUDEA
a scroll in
which he had dictated the
WORDS OF GOD,
the king
ARROGANTLY CUT ITS PAGES
with a knife and threw them
into a **FIREPOT.**

**SO GOD ABANDONED KING JEHOIAKIM,
AND HE WAS TAKEN CAPTIVE AND KILLED
DURING A REBELLION.**

When he became king of Israel,

Jeroboam forgot about obeying God. Instead of altars for God, he expected his people to worship statues of golden calves.

Enter, a prophet of God to call out King Jeroboam's mistake. Of course, he didn't appreciate the prophet's constructive criticism.

King Jeroboam yelled, **"Seize him!"** But as he pointed at the prophet, the king's hand shriveled up.

When King Ahaziah took a bad fall off the palace balcony, he sent messages to the temple of a pagan god.

"Find out if I will recover from this injury."

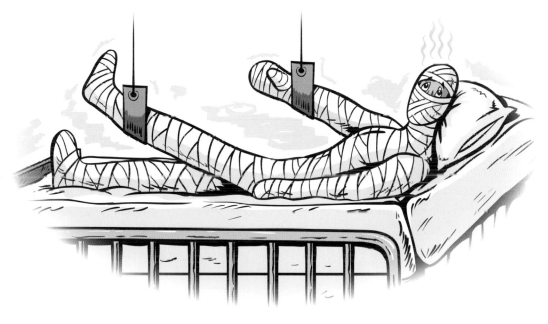

The prophet, **ELIJAH**, intercepted the message and sent word to Ahaziah: "Because you have not turned to **GOD**, you will **NEVER LEAVE** the bed you are lying on."

THE PEOPLE OF ISRAEL
HAD GATHERED AND AGREED TO
ACCEPT REHOBOAM AS THEIR KING,
BUT ONLY ON ONE CONDITION—
THAT HE WOULD LIGHTEN
THE HEAVY BURDENS PUT ON THEM
BY HIS FATHER, KING SOLOMON.

Rehoboam ignored some good advice and did the opposite—he made the people's workloads heavier.

But he misjudged the temper of the people. There was an uproar, and he was promptly dethroned.

Manasseh was only TWELVE YEARS OLD when he became KING OF JUDAH, and he ruled for FIFTY-FIVE YEARS.

HERE'S A LIST OF HIS TOP TEN BAD DEEDS

10. He turned the people away from God and led them to worship pagan gods.

9. He rebuilt the high places (places of pagan worship) that his father, King Hezekiah, had distroyed.

8. He erected altars to Baal and made asherah poles, just as King Ahab had done.

7. He bowed down to all the starry hosts and worshipped them.

6. He built pagan altars in the temple of God.

5. He sacrificed his son.

4. He practiced divination.

3. He sought omens.

2. He consulted mediums and spiritists.

And the **NUMBER ONE** wicked act of King Manasseh ...

He shed so much innocent blood that it would have **FILLED JERUSALEM** from end to end.

Joash

became king of Jerusalem when he was only

seven years old.

For most of his life, he followed God. But then he **lost his way.**

HE DID NOTHING TO STOP THE

IDOL WORSHIP

THAT WAS SPREADING

ACROSS THE COUNTRY,

AND HE HELPED

PLOT THE DEATHS

OF THE PROPHETS

AND PRIESTS, INCLUDING THE

PROPHET ZECHARIAH.

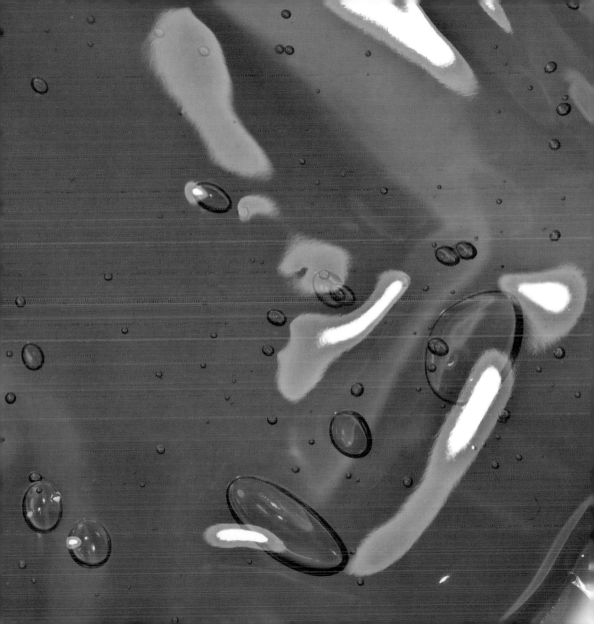

Belshazzar, king of Babylon, liked to throw parties. At one of his **PARTIES,** King Belshazzar got the idea to dig into the **TREASURE TROVE** his father had taken from the temple in Jerusalem—**GOD'S DWELLING PLACE.** As the king and his guests were tipping cups, **GOD'S HAND** appeared out of nowhere and wrote a message on the wall.

Daniel, a prophet from Israel, was brought in to decipher what was clearly a message for

BELSHAZZAR ...

MENE, MENE, TEKEL, PARSIN

MENE: God has limited the time of your rule. He has brought it to an end.

TEKEL: You haven't measured up to God's standard.

PARSIN: Your authority over your kingdom will be taken away from you.

Belshazzar was killed that night.

Achan was there when the Israelites conquered Jericho, and he watched as God helped bring down the city's walls. There was just one ITTY-BITTY INSTRUCTION Achan ignored. God had told the Israelites not to take ANY OF THE RICHES and TREASURES of Jericho for themselves, but something caught Achan's eye.

No one will know if I just nab this really **NICE COAT,** and a few **BARS OF GOLD,** and some **SILVER COINS,** he thought.

ACHAN had a great hiding spot for the loot— **HE BURIED IT IN THE GROUND** under his tent.

No one would see it there— EXCEPT GOD.

THE CONSEQUENCE WAS DEATH.

GEHAZI WAS A SERVANT FOR THE GREAT PROPHET, ELISHA. WHEN ELISHA TURNED DOWN **MONEY** AND **PRESENTS** FROM A MAN FOR **HEALING HIS LEPROSY**, GEHAZI GOT GREEDY. HE RETURNED TO THE NOW-CURED, FORMER **LEPER**, AND THEN HE ASKED FOR THE GIFTS. HE CLAIMED **ELISHA** HAD **CHANGED HIS MIND.**

KING SAUL'S TRAITS

Tall ☑

Handsome ☑

Humble ☑

Compassionate ☑

Self-disciplined ☑

Faithful ☑

Anointed ☑

Chosen by God to be the first king of Israel, Saul took reign at age thirty and ruled over Israel for forty-two years. He was immensely blessed with many fine traits.

Saul had it all! But he threw it all away when he decided he knew better than God. When Saul went to BATTLE against the Amalekites, God told him to wipe them out completely. But Saul kept the best of their ANIMALS and spared the AMALEKITE KING—to humiliate and parade before the Israelites.

And Saul continued to turn away from God in fits of jealousy, SUPERSTITION, and power tripping.

In the end, Saul fell on his OWN SWORD in battle.

When HAMAN was given a seat of honor by the king of Persia, he let it go to his head— which just got BIGGER and BIGGER. Mordecai, adopted dad to the queen, refused to BOW to Haman, and Haman's RAGE turned into a plot to kill Mordecai and ALL THE JEWS.

Haman built a set of **GALLOWS** to hang Mordecai, and then Haman **TRICKED** the king into signing a **DEATH DECREE**. But Haman's **PLAN BACKFIRED**. Instead of killing Mordecai, who had once saved the **KING'S LIFE**, Haman was put to death on his own **GALLOWS**. Mordecai and all the Jews were **SAVED!**

Nabal was a wealthy man, owner of many sheep and goats.

When King David was a fugitive, he and his followers sought refuge in the wilderness. During sheep-shearing season, David sent ten of his men to ask Nabal for food to feed his hungry band of warriors. Instead of assistance, Nabal sent back insults.

In return, David promised, "Not one male belonging to Nabal will be left alive by daybreak!"

But when Nabal's beautiful wife, Abigail, went behind her husband's back to provide food for the men, David withdrew his threat.

TEN DAYS LATER

Nabal died of heart failure, And Abigail married David.

THE MAN WITH THE MANE.

Before Samson was born, an angel came to his mother and told her he would have the strength to save Israel from the Philistines—as long as his hair was never cut.

When he grew up, Samson fell in **LOVE** with a woman named **DELILAH.** She wanted to know where he got all of his **STRENGTH,** but he kept his **LIPS SEALED.** She nagged day after day until he was sick of it. **SAMSON** finally told her about how he'd go weak if his hair was cut.

DELILAH SOLD HIS STRENGTH-SAPPING SECRET TO THE PHILISTINES FOR A PILE OF COINS.

Absalom was another of King David's sons, and he had a celebrity rock star status. He had irresistible charm, dashing good looks, and the best ride in town—a magnificent chariot with horses and fifty men to run in front of it. Absalom was known for his gorgeous skin and long hair. But looks can be deceiving.

Absalom did some icky things:

- **KILLED** his brother Amnon out of revenge.
- **RAN** away and hid for three years.
- **BURNED** a neighbor's barley field.
- **TRIED** to take his father's throne.
- **DROVE** King David out of Jerusalem.
- **WAGED** a war with the king's men.

Again and again,

King David forgave his son's wayward deeds. But Absalom eventually met his fate—in an oak tree. His long, luscious hair got caught in its branches, and King David's soldiers caught him.

The Worm Has Turned

After Jesus' death and ascension, Herod Agrippa I ruled Israel. He had the apostle **JAMES KILLED** and **PETER IMPRISONED**.

HEROD AGRIPPA I GAVE A MOVING SPEECH, AND SOME OF THE PEOPLE HAILED HIM AS A GOD.

But instead of directing the people back to God, Herod soaked up all the praise.

So God struck Herod Agrippa I with nasty **INTESTINAL WORMS** that ate him from the inside out!

I can't believe it!

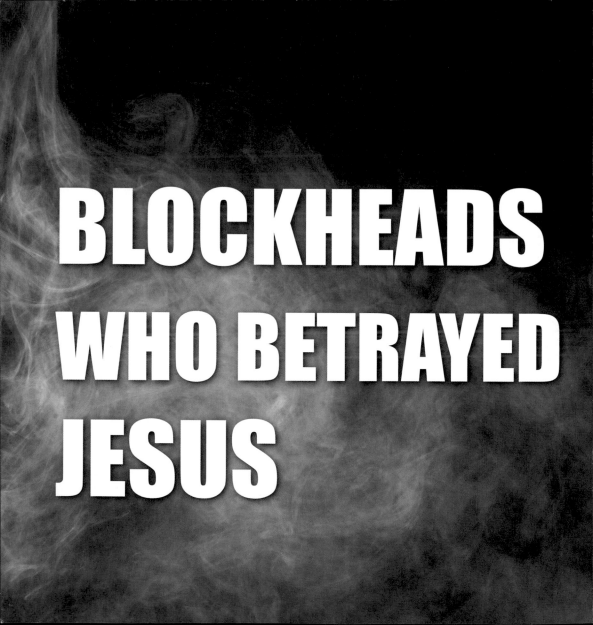

JUDAS WAS ONE OF THE TWELVE DISCIPLES CALLED BY JESUS.

Yet Judas delivered Jesus to the men who would crucify him — for thirty silver coins!

Later, Judas' guilt overwhelmed him, and he returned the bribe money. He knew he'd made a big mistake!

119

Pontius Pilate was in a pickle.

After his betrayal, Jesus was brought to Pontius Pilate, the Roman ruler, to be judged. Pilate's wife had a vision in a dream and warned her husband, "Do not crucify that innocent man!"

Pilate: Which of the two do you want me to release? Barabbas or Jesus?

People: Barabbas.

Pilate: What shall I do then with Jesus who is called the Messiah?

People: Crucify him.

Pilate: Why? What crime has he committed?

People: Crucify him!

Pilate: I am innocent of this man's blood. It is your responsibility!

People: His blood is on us and on our children!

Barabbas was released, and Jesus was handed over to be crucified.

Pilate was afraid to stand up to the people.

So he really wasn't innocent.

121

PETER makes—and breaks—a promise to JESUS.

Right before Jesus was arrested, Peter said he would never disown Jesus. But Jesus predicted that Peter would deny Jesus three times that very night, before the rooster crowed.

Cock-a-doodle-doo!

That night, while Jesus was on trial, Peter turned from faith and dropped into fear. He denied being one of the disciples, not once, not twice, but three times!

After the third denial, a rooster crowed. A WAKE-UP CALL to Peter, perhaps?

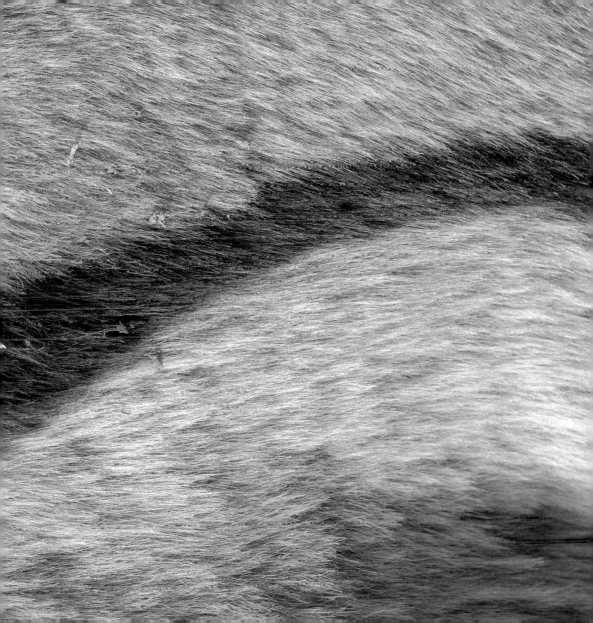

WHEN BALAAM HEADED OUT ON HIS DONKEY to go see the king of Moab, an angel stood in the road to stop him—**THREE TIMES!**

The donkey could see the angel, but Balaam could not, so he prodded and beat his donkey to get it to move. Finally, God opened the donkey's mouth and let it speak to Balaam.

DONKEY: *Hey stop beating me!*
What have I ever done to you?

BALAAM: *You've made a fool of me!*
If I had a sword, I'd kill you.

DONKEY: *Um, how long have I been your donkey?*
Have I ever acted like this before?

And then the angel of the Lord made
himself visible to Balaam.

Balaam fell to the ground and
begged forgivenss. The angel let Balaam pass,
and his donkey forgave him.

127

KING BALAK OF MOAB WAS A MAN WITH A PLAN. HIS PLOT? HE TRIED TO PAY THE PROPHET BALAAM TO PUT A CURSE ON ISRAEL.

JUST ONE GLITCH ....

BALAAM was a prophet of God and could only speak the words God gave him. Balaam's first two messages from God actually **BLESSED** Israel, but Balak kept asking for more. After **SEVEN** prophetic messages that blessed Israel, Balaam **CONVINCED** Balak to give it a rest.

GOD TOLD THE PROPHET JONAH: "GO PREACH TO THE CITY OF NINEVEH."

Nineveh was one scary place, the capital of the Assyrian empire, known for its evil deeds. God wanted Jonah to warn the Ninevites of God's coming judgement. But Jonah ignored God. Here's what happened to Jonah as a result:

- Jonah ran away and boarded a ship bound for Tarshish—a city in the opposite direction of Nineveh.

- God sent a great storm, and the sailors threw Jonah overboard.

- Jonah was swallowed by a huge fish, and he spent three days and nights in the belly of said huge fish.

- Finally the fish vomited Jonah on dry land.

God said to Jonah a second time:

"GO TO NINEVEH AND PREACH."

Jonah:

"ON MY WAY."

FINALLY JONAH WENT OFF TO NINEVEH LIKE GOD TOLD HIM TO DO IN THE FIRST PLACE!

WHAT A BACK STABBER!

Joab was King David's nephew and commander of his army. He was loyal to King David, but he was also a skilled fighter who sometimes took matters into his own hands!

JOAB'S TOP THREE MURDEROUS ACTS:

1 He killed an opposing army commander who was trying to make peace with David.

2 David ordered that his son, Absalom, not be harmed during a rebellion. Joab killed Absalom anyway.

3 After David appointed Amasa as commander in place of Joab, Joab pretended to be Amasa's friend—and then stabbed him to death.

Commander
of the Army

JOAB

and cold-blooded
murderer!

After Solomon was made king, he
ordered Joab to be killed.

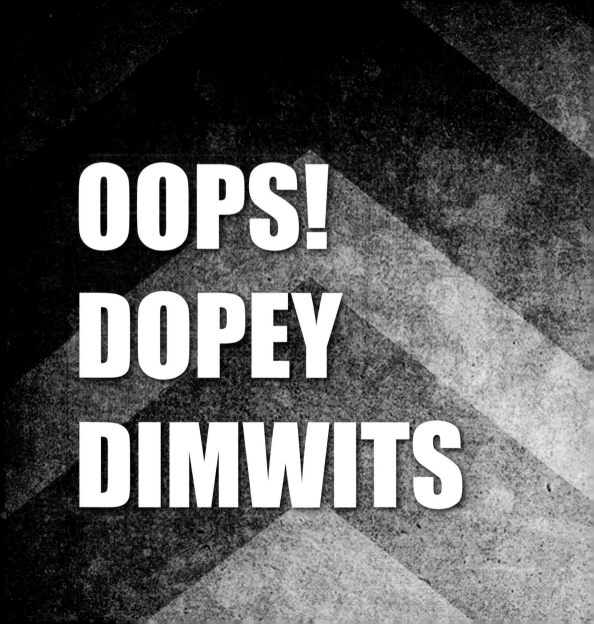

SHIMEI'S FOLLY

King David was **FLEEING** from his son, Absalom, who had taken over David's throne by **TRICKERY.** When David came to Bahurim, Shimei appeared and **THREW ROCKS** and insults at David.

Shimei came from the family of **KING SAUL,** and Shimei **BLAMED** David for Saul's death. When David's throne had been taken by Absalom, Shimei wanted to **RUB DAVID'S NOSE IN IT.**

Fast forward ...

When David regained his thrown, Shimei **HUMBLED** himself (groveled) before the king. David was merciful and spared Shimei but put him under **HOUSE ARREST.**

Jephthah, a great warrior and judge, got a little carried away.

Jephthah prepared for battle by making a vow to God that if he were successful, he would give as a burnt offering whatever should come out of his house first to greet him upon his return.

Of course, he figured it would be one of his many animals— **NOT HIS DAUGHTER!** Jephthah won the battle, but when he got home, the first to greet him was his only child. Oh, no!

The Bible says Jephthah kept his vow to God, but instead of sacrificing her, some Bible experts say he set his daugther apart for a life of singleness and worship to God.

KORAH AND HIS BUDDIES **DATHAN** AND **ABIRAM**—AND A GROUP OF **250** MEN, **COMPLAINED** AND ROSE UP **AGAINST** MOSES AND AARON AND SAID TO THEM:

What makes you better than us?

But Moses and Aaron had done everything the Lord had commanded. God told Moses to warn the people to move far away from Korah's, Dathan's, and Abiram's tents—like far, far away.

BOOM

The ground split open and swallowed them.

With friends like these ... who needs enemies?

Job, who was **RESPECTED** by all, was a good man and considered least likely to have any **FRENEMIES.** But he had three: Eliphaz, Bildad, and Zophar.

Job's buddies saw how **BAD** life had gotten for him—he'd lost his **PROPERTY**, his possessions, his **WEALTH**, even his children—and they had no idea what to say. For a week they **SAT WITH JOB** and kept their mouths shut. But then they just couldn't hold back. **INSTEAD OF COMFORTING** Job, they ganged up on him! "Admit your sin," they said. "That's why all this bad stuff is happening to you."

Nothing could shake Job's **FAITH IN GOD.** "What a bunch of **MISERABLE** comforters! Is there no end to your **WINDBAG SPEECHES?**" Job said to them.

TAKE THAT!

God rebuked the trio of troublemakers and told them they'd better beg Job to pray for them.

The prophet Elisha was just minding his own business, walking along the road to Bethel, when a **HUGE** gang of boys approached him.

Hey, baldy! Get out of here, baldy!

HECKLING a prophet is not the best move. Elisha called down a **CURSE** from heaven, and two wild **BEARS** came out of the woods and **ATE FORTY-TWO BOYS** for lunch.

147

Love thy neighbor?

THE PEOPLE OF AMMON, JUST EAST OF ISRAEL, **JUMPED** UP AND DOWN WITH JOY WHEN THEIR **NEIGHBORS** WERE **EXILED** FROM THE HOLY LAND.

Whoop!-Whoop!

BUT NOT BECAUSE THEY WERE SHOWING OVERWHELMING NEIGHBORLY LOVE AND SUPPORT.

They STAMPED THEIR FEET, CLAPPED THEIR HANDS, CHEERED, and JEERED at God's people, the Israelites. So God WIPED OUT the Ammonites from the earth.

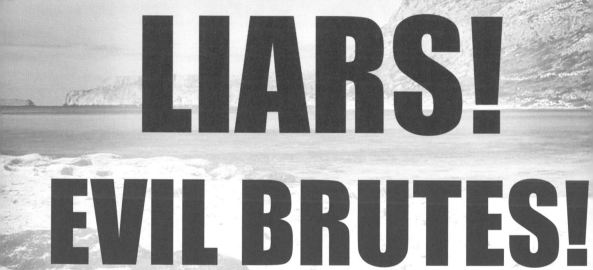

The people of the island of **CRETE** had a notoriously **BAD** reputation!

LIARS!

EVIL BRUTES!

GLUTTONS!

Those are some harsh words, but the apostle Paul referred to the Cretans as

"DETESTABLE, DISOBEDIENT, and UNFIT FOR DOING ANYTHING GOOD."

Pharisees were a **RELIGIOUS SOCIETY,** and they were sticklers for **RULES.** They didn't like it when Jesus was friendly with SINNERS, and they were constantly quizzing him. They tried to **STUMP** him with questions about sinners, the **SABBATH, FORGIVENESS,** and more.

ON TOTAL ACCEPTANCE AND UNCONDITIONAL LOVE:

PHARISEES: Why do you hang out with sinners?

JESUS: It is not the healthy who need a doctor.

ON NOT WORKING DURING THE SABBATH:

PHARISEES: Why do you perform unlawful healings on our day of rest?

JESUS: It is lawful to do good any day, even on the Sabbath.

ON THE POWER OF FORGIVENESS:

PHARISEES: Is it not true that only God has the power to forgive?

JESUS: The Son of Man has the authority to forgive.

Bad-itude instead of Gratitude!

God miraculously delivered the Israelites from Egyptian slavery. He parted the Red Sea to help them escape into the Promised Land. He provided water from rocks in the desert. He led them by pillars of cloud and fire. He provided daily food. Pretty awesome stuff! But as soon as the Israelites got hungry, thirsty, tired, or weary, they griped and complained.

God kept sending miracles

to remind them that they were cared for and loved, but they continued to be ungrateful. The Israelites lacked nothing, except for unshakable gratitude and rock-solid faith in God.

WE ARE ALL BLOCKHEADS ...

Sometimes anyway.
We all have blockhead
moments, each and every
one of us. But God loves
us and provides grace
and forgiveness.

He uses our lives (even our mistakes) for his glory. To learn more about the blockheads featured in this book, check out God's Word—the Bible.

You'll see God loves us, mistakes and all.

Scripture Index

Sources

Baker, Anisa, ed., *801 Questions Kids Ask About God with Answers from the Bible.* Carol Stream: Tyndale House Publishers, 2000.

Lockyer, Herbert, *All the Men/All the Women of the Bible Compilation*. Grand Rapids: Zondervan, 2006.

Rasmussen, Carl G., *Zondervan Atlas of the Bible, Revised Edition*. Grand Rapids: Zondervan, 2010.

Strauss, Ed, *Seriously Sick Bible Stuff, 2:52 Series*. Grand Rapids: Zondervan, 2007.

Tenney, Merrill C., Silva, Moises, editors, *The Zondervan Encyclopedia of the Bible, Revised Edition, Volume 5*. Grand Rapids: 2009.

Zondervan Publishing, *NIV Boys' Bible.* Grand Rapids: Zondervan, 2012.

Zondervan Publishing, *NIV Quest Study Bible*. Grand Rapids: Zondervan, 2011.